For

Mom H.

with congratulations and

best wishes on your

birthday

from

Haubenstricht's

Dec. 16, *19* 98

Teach us to number our days, that we may apply our hearts unto wisdom.
                            —Psalm 90:12

A Birthday Remembrance

Louis O. Caldwell

*Drawings
by
Leonardo M. Ferguson*

Abingdon
Nashville

A BIRTHDAY REMEMBRANCE

Copyright © 1977 by Abingdon

All rights in this book are reserved. No part of the book may be reproduced in any manner whatsoever without written permission of the publisher except brief quotations embodied in critical articles or reviews. For information address Abingdon,

Nashville, Tennessee.

Library of Congress Cataloging in Publication Data

Caldwell, Louis O
  A birthday remembrance.

  1. Christian life—1960– 2. Birthdays.
I. Title.
BV4501.2.C24   248'.4   77-7043

ISBN 0-687-03555-4

The prayer on page 42 was first published in *Reader's Digest* (March, 1959) with the following identification: "Former Gov. Thomas E. Dewey of New York likes to quote this prayer sent to him by William E. Robinson, who, in turn, received it from its author, a Mother Superior who wishes to be anonymous."
The poem on page 46 is "Prayer" by Henry van Dyke from *The Poems of Henry van Dyke* (copyright 1911 Charles Scribner's Sons) is reprinted by permission of Charles Scribner's Sons.
The poem on page 50 is "The Day—The Way" by John Oxenham from *Bees in Amber*. Used by permission of Miss Theo Oxenham.
The quotation on page 59 is from "The Philosopher" by Sara Teasdale, used by permission of the Literary Executor of Miss Teasdale's estate, Margaret Conklin.
In a very few cases, where copyright may still subsist, it has proved impossible to trace the present copyright holders, if any, and in such cases, it is hoped that the omission will be excused.

MANUFACTURED BY THE PARTHENON PRESS AT
NASHVILLE, TENNESSEE, UNITED STATES OF AMERICA.

To the memory of my maternal grandfather,
Oliver Wendell McDonald
and my uncle,
The Reverend Thomas Louis Spiers

A good man leaveth an inheritance to his children's children.
—*Proverbs 13:22*

Preface

"How old art thou?" This familiar question has its earliest biblical recording in Genesis, the book of the beginnings. The question was asked Jacob by Pharaoh, who received this reply: "The days of the years of my pilgrimage are an hundred and thirty years."

Whether this episode happened on Jacob's birthday, it does contain an intriguing starting point for a book for those who *are* celebrating their birthday. Adding another candle to one's birthday cake causes all but the most undiscerning and insensitive to reflect on the meaning of the days of our pilgrimage. In fact, a birthday could be defined as an annual pause in our pilgrimage, a special time for reflection, celebration, and anticipation!

This book has been prepared for the purpose of providing some brief thoughts appropriate to this special occasion. If the reader finds in this little volume something that gives a lift for the living of the days of the pilgrimage, I will be grateful to him whose pilgrimage points the way.

I wish to thank Patsy Moss and Pam Werden, who not only typed the manuscript but offered encouragement as well.

And of course I want to personally wish you the kind of pause that will be productive to the pilgrim and the pilgrimage!

Louis O. Caldwell

Contents

Some Thoughts on
Celebrating Your Birthday *13*

The Pause

1. Pause for Perspective *19*
2. The Pause That Renews *23*
3. The Key to Prosperity and Success *27*

The Pilgrim

4. Look in the Mirror *33*
5. A Reminder of Your Value *37*
6. As the Candles Add Up *41*

The Pilgrimage

7. The Journey and Its Secret *47*
8. Companion for the Pilgrimage *51*
9. Live All the Days of Your Life *55*
10. Fully Alive *59*

A Birthday Prayer *62*

Some Thoughts on Celebrating Your Birthday

To be remembered on one's birthday is an experience that most of us value highly. Although some pretend otherwise, I believe that we value this kind of remembrance more with the passing of time, for to be remembered when another candle is added to the birthday cake means that someone cares and that our lives have significance for that person.

Few needs of the human heart are as great as that of experiencing a sense of importance. One's birthday provides a unique opportunity for us to realize that at a certain time and place in the history of events the human family increased by one. Another thread woven into the fabric of mankind, and the fabric is never the same from that moment! It is no wonder then that all days on the calendar do not have the same importance. The day of our birth should remind us that we do indeed matter.

Perhaps there is no thought more repugnant to the mind than to think that we are born, live out our days, and then pass from this life without having made some important difference to someone.

So as you pause on this special day, think of the esteem in which others hold you. Allow these thoughts to enrich and inspire you. Among the most gratifying achievements of life is to have secured a place in the thoughts and affections of those who remember you on this day.

From Genesis through Revelation, the sacred

pages of Scripture teach the celebration of life. Our Judeo-Christian heritage stresses that God is the source and sustainer of all life and that as recipients of the breath of life we glorify God by living celebratively with a sense of reverence. Therefore, to celebrate your birthday is to engage in a distinctly Christian practice!

The Pause

And he said unto them, Come ye yourselves apart . . . and rest a while.

—*Mark 6:31*

Even the youths shall faint and be weary, and the young men shall utterly fall: But they that wait upon the Lord shall renew their strength; they shall mount up with wings as eagles; they shall run, and not be weary; and they shall walk, and not faint.
—*Isaiah 40:30-31*

A man of meditation is happy, not for an hour or a day, but quite round the circle of all his years.
—*Isaac Taylor*

All men's miseries derive from not being able to sit quiet in a room alone.
—*Blaise Pascal*

Pause for Perspective

There is something about a birthday that calls to mind the celebrated statement of Solomon's found in Ecclesiastes: "To every thing there is a season, and a time to every purpose under the heaven." A birthday should be a time for productive pausing.

When we study the life of Christ, we observe that pauses were a vital part of his earthly life. In John's Gospel for example, we read that "he departed again into a mountain himself alone."

Notice the word "again" in John's observation. Why did Jesus pause in his busy schedule and find what to him was sacred solitude? Although we may never enter fully into the answer, we can follow his example and discover how productive the right kind of pause can be.

We know, for example, that a productive pause can restore and enlarge perspective. Remember the scene in Lewis Carroll's *Alice Through the Looking-Glass* when the Red Queen has poor Alice by the hand and, pulling her along, keeps crying "Faster! Faster!"? Alice observes that they have made no progress and gets an explanation that sounds remarkably like one of contemporary life. "Here, you see," explains the Queen, "it takes all the running you can do, to keep in the same place. If you want to get somewhere else, you must run at least twice as fast as that!"

A friend of James Truslow Adams, the noted historian, was a distinguished explorer who spent some time among the natives of the upper Amazon. Once he related to Adams a lesson he learned when he and a group of natives attempted a forced march through the jungle. For the first two days the party made extraordinary progress; but on the third morning, instead of preparing to start at the appointed time, all the natives were found sitting on their haunches looking very solemn and showing no sense of haste. When the explorer asked the chief for an explanation, the chief replied, "They are waiting. They cannot move farther until their souls have caught up with their bodies."

Perhaps we inhabitants of the concrete jungle have some lessons to learn about productive pausing!

The hectic pace of modern life can cause us to lose our perspective, resulting in a loss of zest and sense of direction. In productive pausing we can pray:

> Drop thy still dews of quietness,
> Till all our strivings cease,
> Take from our souls the strain and stress,
> And let our ordered lives confess
> The beauty of thy peace.
> —*John Greenleaf Whittier*

He leadeth me beside the still waters.
—*Psalm 23:2*

It is not hasty reading, but seriously meditating upon holy and heavenly truths that makes them prove sweet and profitable to the soul. It is not the bee's touching on the flowers that gathers the honey, but her abiding for a time upon them, and drawing out the sweet. It is not he that reads most, but he that meditates most on divine truth, that will prove the choicest, wisest, strongest Christian.
—*Joseph Hall, Bishop of Norwich*

Reading and conversation may furnish us with many ideas of men and things, yet it is our own meditation that must form our judgment.
—*Isaac Watts*

The Pause That Renews

In a letter to his young niece, John Ruskin wrote: "There's no music in a rest, Katie, that I know of, but there's the making of music in it. And people are always missing that part of the life melody."

No one knew more about the music of rest in life's melody than the psalmist David. He learned the importance of the pause and scattered the word *selah*—meaning "pause"—throughout the book of Psalms. Seventy-five times we find the word *selah* in verses that have inspired readers over the centuries. Known as a man after God's own heart, David knew the importance of pausing, pondering, reflecting, and meditating. He, like few others, understood that maintaining a proper perspective on life requires occasional pauses that help us understand the relation of our personal experiences to the total scheme of things. As David reminds us, "God is our refuge and strength, a very present help in trouble."

The *selah* in life's melody ought to provide us with the chance to raise the level of our living, for most of us are wanting not more days in our lives, but more life in our days. Sir William Osler, one of the world's great physicians, used to say that "failure to cultivate the power of peaceful concentration is the greatest single cause of mental breakdown." And William James, the American pioneer of psychology, believed that "neither the nature nor the amount of our work is accountable for the frequency and severity of our breakdowns. Their cause lies rather in those absurd feelings of hurry and having no time, in that breathlessness and tension . . . that lack of harmony and ease."

Productive pausing *can* be a part of our busy, modern way of life. One of the most beautiful descriptions of this *selah* experience is given us by Grace Watkins in her poem "The Green Place":

> Lord, may there be a still green place
> For everyone . . . a little pool
> Within a forest where the lace
> Of ferns is delicate and cool;
> A meadow where across the grass
> Small clover-scented breezes pass. . . .
>
> And, Lord, if there are those for whom
> There is no quiet retreat,
> Oh, let a healing memory bloom
> To bring a refreshment deep and sweet
> And please, Lord, keep it very green
> However long the years between.

O how I love thy law! it is my meditation all the day.

—*Psalm 119:97*

Meditation is the life of the soul; action is the soul of meditation; honor is the reward of action: so meditate, that thou mayst do; so do, that thou mayst purchase honor; for which purchase, give God the glory.

—*Francis Quarles*

It is not the number of books you read, nor the variety of sermons you hear, nor the amount of religious conversation in which you mix, but it is the frequency and earnestness with which you meditate on these things till the truth in them becomes your own and part of your being, that ensures your growth.

—*F. W. Robertson*

The Key to Prosperity and Success

If we use the Bible and the life of Christ as our authority, we learn that productive pausing is a vital aspect of an effective pattern of living. Nevertheless, meditation is not well understood.

Meditation cannot be understood apart from its object, and we are told in the Scriptures what the proper object is. In preparing the Israelites for the conquest of Canaan, Joshua instructed them: "This book of the law shall not depart out of thy mouth; but thou shalt meditate therein day and night, that thou mayest observe to do according to all that is written therein: for then thou shalt make thy way prosperous, and then thou shalt have good success" (Joshua 1:8). Defined by scripture, meditation that prepares us for prosperous and successful living is (1) based on the eternal word of God, the Bible, (2) practiced consistently, and (3) expressed by active obedience.

When practiced according to scriptural guidelines, meditation produces amazing discoveries. A few years ago, a prominent psychoanalyst addressed a Canadian audience and afterward was asked for a practical solution to the problems of living. Promptly came this reply: "Quietness. The experience of stillness. You have to be able to stop in order to be able to change direction." In the quietness of Bible-based meditation, a person can discover many other things—the need to change, the need to act, the need to set new goals.

Think of the discovery made by the author of the following:

> Softly I closed the Book as in a dream
> And let its echoes linger to redeem
> Silence with music, darkness with its gleam.
>
> That day I worked no more. I could not bring
> My hands to toil, my thoughts to trafficking.
> A new light shone on every common thing.
>
> Celestial glories flamed before my gaze.
> That day I worked no more. But, to God's praise,
> I shall work better all my other days.
> —*Winfred Ernest Garrison*

If this kind of experience can come from meditating on *a* book, consider the possibilities in meditating on *the* book!

The Pilgrim

The Lord sent thee on a journey.
—I Samuel 15:18

And Moses said unto God, Who am I . . . ?
—*Exodus 3:11*

You've no idea what a poor opinion I have of myself, and how little I deserve it.
—*William S. Gilbert*

If I were to search for the central core of difficulty in people as I have come to know them, it is that in the great majority of cases they despise themselves, regarding themselves worthless and unlovable.
—*Carl R. Rogers*

Look in the Mirror

After practicing psychiatry for over forty years, Smiley Blanton said that most of the people who sought his help were neither the very young nor the very old. They were in their middle years, often in their thirties or forties. Instead of living more fully and joyously, they were confused, frustrated, and unhappy.

What was holding them back? They were holding themselves back. But Dr. Blanton believed that it was possible to change the pattern of living that led his patients into such misery. He said that "people can and do change when something or somebody gives them new insight into themselves."

To achieve this deeper understanding of self, Dr. Blanton urges people to deliberately take time to ask themselves certain questions: Who am I? What made me this way? Where am I going? Where do I want to go?

We discover ourselves in the inspired pages of Holy Scripture. More truthfully, we can say that apart from this book, we do not know how to think of ourselves. We literally learn who we are and how to understand ourselves by reading the Bible. As the psalmist wrote, "Thy word is a lamp unto my feet, and a light to my path."

How does the Bible teach us to think of ourselves? In the Old Testament, the venerable heroes of faith—Abel, Enoch, Noah, and Abraham, to name only a few—are identified in the great faith chapter, the eleventh chapter of the book of Hebrews.

According to the author of Hebrews, these godly adventurers died without receiving God's promises, but they embraced them nevertheless and lived in the belief of their reality. Their remarkable lives can largely be explained in terms of how they viewed themselves. This fascinating insight is given us in the thirteenth verse: They "confessed that they were strangers and pilgrims on the earth."

New Testament Christians are addressed in identical language. "I beseech you," wrote Peter, "as strangers and pilgrims . . ." (I Peter 2:11). Thus we find both Old Testament servants of God and New Testament believers in Christ described as "strangers and pilgrims." To understand ourselves in this way is to achieve an identity that radically affects the whole of life. For as it is given us in Scripture, the pilgrims "desire a better country, that is, an heavenly"; and the astonishing result is: "wherefore God is not ashamed to be called their God: for he hath prepared for them a city" (Hebrews 11:16).

Many of us have sung the old familiar hymn whose lyrics celebrate the pilgrim identity:

> This world is not my home
> I'm just a passing through.

The scriptural way of thinking about ourselves enables us to live effectively in the world because we are not confined to it. Christians are truly contemporary as by-products of the pilgrim identity that places their citizenship beyond time and space.

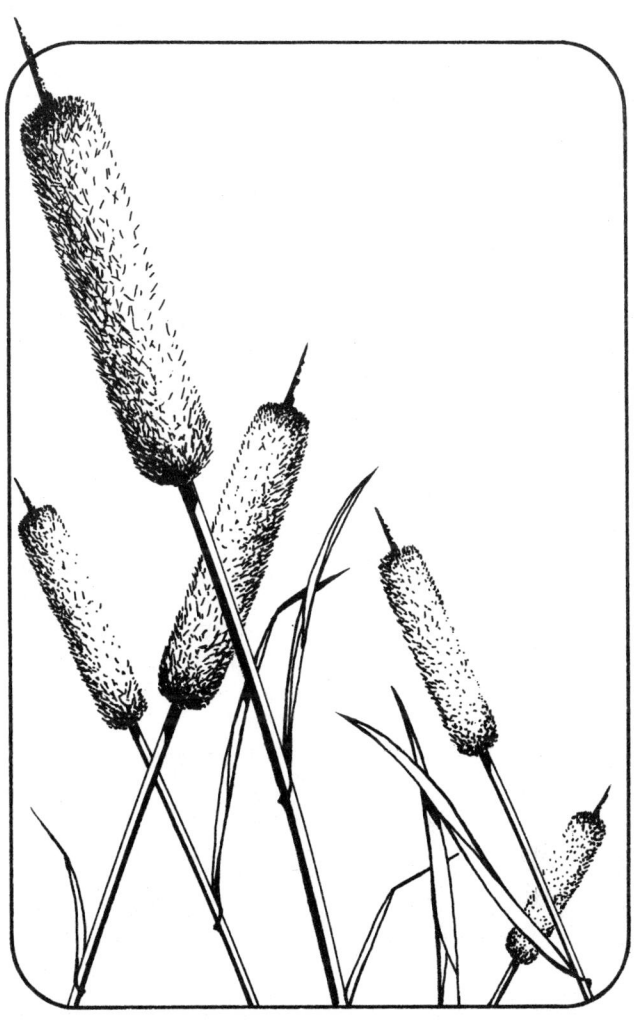

What is man, that thou art mindful of him?
—Psalm 8:4

Consider
The lilies of the field, whose bloom is brief—
　We are as they;
　Like them we fade away,
　　As doth a leaf.

Consider
The sparrows of the air, of small account:
　Our God doth view
Whether they fall or mount—
　He guards us too.

Consider
The lilies, that do neither spin nor toil,
　Yet are most fair—
　What profits all this care,
　　And all this coil?

Consider
The birds, that have no barn nor harvest-weeks:
　God gives them food—
Much more our Father seeks
　To do us good.

　　　　　　　　　　　—*Christina Rossetti*

In the reality of life, the pages are turned only one at a time, each at its proper time, and not before.
　　　　　　　　　　　—*Paul Tournier*

To be happy, we must be true to nature and carry our age along with us.

　　　　　　　　　　　—*William Hazlitt*

A Reminder of Your Value

A teacher assigned his class an autobiographical essay. When the papers had been graded and given back to the pupils, one boy reacted strongly. With paper in hand, he walked up to the teacher and said, "I would like to know what right you have to rate my entire life as a B-minus?"

That paper's young author believed his life was more important than the teacher's grade indicated—and so do we! John Wesley certainly would have agreed. Methodism's founder used to require each of the early Methodist preachers to write the story of his soul's pilgrimage. Frank W. Boreham, who preached and wrote the Christian message so winsomely for more than thirty years, believed that "the man whose biography is not worth writing has never yet been born." Deep in every human heart is a yearning for a sense of personal significance. William James used to tell his students at Harvard that the deepest need of a person is the need to be appreciated.

Life is supremely worth living when we feel that we can make a significant contribution, that we matter! John Tyndale, the English scientist, often spoke fondly of the elderly man who attended him. Each morning the old gentleman would knock on the famous professor's door and say, "Arise, sir. It is near seven o'clock. You have great work to do this day!"

The deepest truth regarding the worth of a person is found in God's estimate of human creation: "For God so loved the world, that he gave his only begotten Son, that whosoever believeth in him should not perish, but have everlasting life." Thus the pilgrim's sense of significance is *derived*. Where does this value of personal worth come from? This is a critical question because it points to the need for identifying the proper reason for celebrating personal significance.

In the Eighth Psalm, David asks, "What is man, that thou art mindful of him?" Properly understood, this is an exclamation as well as a question. When the psalmist asks "What is man?" he is not disparaging mankind, rather the psalmist is filled with wonder because we are the object of God's attention. David marveled because, of all God's creative work, *persons* occupy a place of uniqueness in the total scheme of things. "For thou hast made him a little lower than the angels, and hast crowned him with glory and honour. Thou madest him to have dominion over the works of thy hands; thou hast put all things under his feet: All sheep and oxen, yea, and beasts of the field; the fowl of the air, and the fish of the sea, and whatsoever passeth through the paths of the seas."

Later the son of God would come to this world and declare this awe-inspiring mindfulness of God, not just for mankind, but for you and me individually. Jesus asked, "Are not two sparrows sold for a farthing? and one of them shall not fall on the ground without your Father. But the very hairs of your head are all numbered. Fear ye not therefore, ye are of more value than many sparrows" (Matthew 10:29-31).

The path of the just is as the shining light, that shineth more and more unto the perfect day.
—Proverbs 4:18

Some men never seem to grow old. Always active in thought, always ready to adopt new ideas, they are never chargeable with fogyism. Satisfied, yet ever dissatisfied, settled, yet ever unsettled, they always enjoy the best of what is, and are the first to find the best of what will be.

—*Anonymous*

To be seventy years young is sometimes far more cheerful and hopeful than to be forty years old.
—*Oliver Wendell Holmes*

I've found a formula for avoiding
All of aging's plaguing fears.
If I take proper care of each day.
Then the calendar takes care of the years!
—*Louis O. Caldwell*

As the Candles Add Up

Perhaps the thought of aging would take on more attractive features if we considered the biblical pattern. The concept of aging scripturally makes the untraveled road look appealing indeed!

Life is brief.
What is your life? It is even a vapour, that appeareth for a little time, and then vanisheth away.
—*James 4:14*

Strength is given in proportion to the length of life.
As thy days, so shall thy strength be.
—*Deuteronomy 33:25*

The Christian pattern of living gets better with the passing of time.
The path of the just is as the shining light, that shineth more and more unto the perfect day.
—*Proverbs 4:18*
The Lord shall increase you more and more.
—*Psalm 115:14*
The righteous also shall hold in his way, and he that hath clean hands shall be stronger and stronger.
—*Job 17:9*

As we get older we can depend upon God's continual care.
I have been young, and now am old; yet have I not seen the righteous forsaken.
—*Psalm 37:25*

The growing, expanding life is the will of God.
We beseech you, brethren, that ye increase more and more.

—*I Thessalonians 4:10*

Be ye also enlarged.

—*II Corinthians 6:13*

Whatever our age, we will continue to grow in the finest sense of that word if we can make the following our prayer:

> Lord, Thou knowest better than I know myself that I am growing older, and will some day be old.
>
> Keep me from getting talkative, and particularly from the fatal habit of thinking I must say something on every subject and on every occasion.
>
> Release me from craving to try to straighten out everybody's affairs.
>
> Keep my mind free from the recital of endless details—give me wings to get to the point. . . .
>
> Teach me the glorious lesson that occasionally it is possible that I may be mistaken.
>
> Keep me reasonably sweet; I do not want to be a saint—some of them are so hard to live with—but a sour old woman [or a crotchety old man] is one of the crowning works of the devil.
>
> Make me thoughtful, but not moody; helpful, but not bossy. With my vast store of wisdom, it seems a pity not to use it all—but Thou knowest, Lord, that I want a few friends at the end.
>
> —*Anonymous*

The Pilgrimage

*The steps of a good man are ordered by the L*ORD.
—*Psalm 37:23*

Give me my scallop-shell of quiet,
My staff of faith to walk upon,
My scrip of joy, immortal diet,
My bottle of salvation:
My gown of glory, hope's true gage,
And thus I'll take my pilgrimage.
—*Sir Walter Raleigh*

Lord, the newness of this day
Calls me to an untried way:
Let me gladly take the road,
Give me strength to bear my load,
Thou my guide and helper be—
I will travel through with Thee.
—*Henry van Dyke*

Every age has its own adventure.
—*Paul Tournier*

The Journey and Its Secret

One day a stranger approached Socrates and asked, "How do I find Mount Olympus?"

"Make every step you take go in that direction," replied the sage.

The wise Greek philosopher knew that if life is to be lived well, it must be lived *directionally*. But which direction? Modern man is much like the pilot who announced to his passengers, "We're lost, but we're making good time!"

Amid the confusion of our time, we are in desperate need of hearing the startling but clear declaration of Jesus who said, "I am the way." The early followers of Christ were known as people of the Way. They had learned to think of life as a special kind of journey, a pilgrimage. But how is this pilgrimage best traveled? The longer one has journeyed, the more one realizes that the final answers to such questions lie in part beyond the reach of even the most brilliant mind.

A hint of what we are looking for is contained in a Persian fairy tale, "Three Princes of Serendip." Serendip was the Arabic name for the island we know as Ceylon. According to the legend, the kingdom of Serendip was under the reign of a powerful monarch named Fafer, who was the proud father of three very promising sons. In his careful preparation of these sons, Fafer not only personally instructed them, but sent them out to travel into other lands. As they traveled they learned many things that they were not directly seeking to learn.

This experience was called *serendipity* by Sir Horace Walpole in the eighteenth century. *The American College Dictionary* defines it as "the faculty of making desirable but unsought-for discoveries by accident."

The term *serendipity* suggests that if the central aim is right, the principle of serendipity will operate accordingly. Who will tell us what life's central aim is? Christians believe that Jesus gave the world the greatest statement on purpose and by-products. He said, "Seek ye first the kingdom of God, and his righteousness; and all these things shall be added unto you" (Matthew 6:33). By "all these things," Jesus was referring to those necessities of life that persons mistakenly set up as primary aims. He was not chiding the people for being concerned with these things, for he clearly understood these needs. The profound truth is, he was showing that by seeking first the kingdom of God and his righteousness, these human needs will be met as a by-product.

As people of the Way, space-age Christians continue the historic pilgrimage. Our experiences continue to confirm the statement of the sixth-century missionary, Brendan. Making his appearance at the court of the Pictish King Brude, he preached the gospel of Christ. At the conclusion of the sermon, the king asked, "Supposing I accept your gospel, what shall I find?" Brendan's reply is memorable: "You will stumble on wonder upon wonder, and every wonder true."

Lo, I am with you alway, even unto the end of the world.

—*Matthew 28:20*

Not for one single day
Can I discern my way,
    But this I surely know—
Who gives the day
Will show the way,
    So I securely go.
        —John Oxenham

Earth's crammed with heaven,
And every common bush afire with God;
But only he who sees, takes off his shoes,
The rest sit round it and pluck blackberries,
And daub their natural faces unaware
More and more from the first similitude.
        —Elizabeth Barrett Browning

Companion for the Pilgrimage

Lovers of John Masefield's poetry are sometimes surprised to learn that he also wrote a play entitled *The Trial of Jesus.* In it a conversation takes place between the wife of Pontius Pilate and the centurion who had been in charge of Christ's execution:

> "Do you think he is dead?"
> "No, Lady, I don't."
> "Then where is he?"
> "Let loose in the world, where neither Roman nor Jew can stop his truth."

The centurion's insight explains why the Christian's pilgrimage through this world is different from that of all others. *The Christian never walks alone.* Shortly after his resurrection, Christ majestically and triumphantly declared, "I am with you alway, even unto the end of the world." We believe with Malcolm Muggeridge, "Either Jesus never was or he still is."

In Philadelphia, in the heart of Temple University, the famous Chapel of Four Chaplains is located within the walls and under the sanctuary of the Baptist Temple. It was conceived by David A. Poling, the father of Clark Poling, one of the four chaplains for whom the chapel was named. These chaplains were aboard the aircraft carrier *Dorchester* when she was torpedoed, and sank in the Atlantic during World War II. All four of these men gave their life preservers to others as the ship went down. Survivors recalled their last sight of the four—they had joined hands and were praying and singing as the ship went down. As Chaplain Poling was preparing to embark on that ill-fated mission, he wrote letters to his family and to his parents. In both letters he included these lines: "I know I shall have your prayers; but please don't pray simply that God will keep me safe. War is a dangerous business. Pray that God will make me adequate!" No one could question whether that prayer for adequacy was answered!

Living the days of our pilgrimage, each one of us is called upon to face life in ways that expose our human inadequacy. If by the biblical exercising of our faith, we have come into a living relationship with Christ, however, we have more than adequate resources for the journey. As one who tested this truth wrote: "I know both how to be abased, and I know how to abound: every where and in all things I am instructed both to be full and to be hungry, both to abound and to suffer need. I can do all things through Christ which strengtheneth me." And having learned this victorious pattern of living, Paul could say to all believers in every generation: "My God shall supply all your need according to his riches in glory by Christ Jesus" (Philippians 4:12-13, 19).

When we come into a scripturally defined relationship with the living Christ, we receive from this relationship that which codes and creeds can never give. Ideals and rational guidelines for living can never completely substitute for the *personal* relationship. It was because those early disciples had personally encountered the living Christ, to whom all power in heaven and in earth had been given, that they "turned the world upside down."

Day unto day uttereth speech.
—Psalm 19:2

> Build today, then, strong and sure,
>   With a firm and ample base;
> And ascending and secure
>   Shall tomorrow find its place.
> —*Henry Wadsworth Longfellow*

Only that day dawns to which we are awake.
—*Henry David Thoreau*

Nothing is more highly to be prized than the value of each day.
—*Johann Wolfgang von Goethe*

One of the illusions of life is that the present hour is not the critical, decisive hour. Write it on your heart that every day is the best day of the year.
—*Ralph Waldo Emerson*

Live All the Days of Your Life

William Lyon Phelps, the Christian educator who taught so brilliantly at Yale for more than thirty years, believed that our attitude toward birthdays revealed basic beliefs about life in general.

On his birthday English satirist Jonathan Swift would wear black mourning clothes and fast the entire day to show how much he regretted being born. Yet, Swift evidently yearned for a more positive, fulfilling life, for he wrote, "May you live all the days of your life."

If we are to live all the days of our life, we must learn the secret of the psalmist David: "This is the day which the LORD hath made; we will rejoice and be glad in it." Getting the most out of life requires living fully in the present.

Too many are like the Indian poet Tagore who lamented, "I have spent my days stringing and unstringing my instrument, while the song I came to sing remains unsung."

> I plan for the future.
> I yearn for the past.
> And, meantime, the present
> Is leaving me fast.

This is the day the Lord has made. The sacred gift of life is given us one day at a time. We are gaining a true understanding of how to live fully when we realize the supreme importance of the present. Only when life is lived now, in harmony with God's will, do we experience life yielding the kind of meaning that makes the pilgrim truly enjoy the pilgrimage.

I am come that they might have life, and that they might have it more abundantly.

—*John 10:10*

The more we live, more brief appear
Our life's succeeding stages:
A day to childhood seems a year,
And years like passing ages.
—*Thomas Campbell*

Life has meaning for me only if it remains a perpetual becoming, a definite goal in front of one and not behind.

—*George Bernard Shaw*

Success is always possible for a person who will look not back, but forward.

—*Paul Tournier*

Fully Alive

In the second century lived a man named Irenaeus who would have added spice to any birthday celebration. He once declared boldly that "the glory of God is a man fully alive!"

I'm sure that Irenaeus and my maternal grandfather would have had some great times together. On his eightieth birthday my grandpa McDonald and I sat talking on the screened-in porch of his old farmhouse in Morales, Texas. For more than thirty-five years this place in the country had drawn so many of us to enjoy special occasions together. I am certain that our reasons for returning went beyond the occasions themselves.

In so many ways Grandpa reminded me of the kind of man Sara Teasdale wrote about in her poem "The Philosopher." She pictured him sitting "as old men do" and pointed out his age (ninety-two) and how he had experienced a long, eventful life. Although his journey had been lengthy, he had never lost that special brightness in his eyes, despite having looked at "three graves on the hill." When she asked him how he had managed to keep his eyes bright with life, he gave this memorable reply:

> I make the most of all that comes,
> The least of all that goes.

Evidently Grandpa had developed that kind of philosophy, for at eighty his mind was as keen and hungry for knowledge as it had been when I knew him as a boy. That is why I had planned to ask him a special question at this birthday reunion. After dinner, the right time finally came. I asked with great anticipation, "Grandpa, you have lived a full, rich life and have learned many things. In your eighty years what has been the most important lesson you have ever learned?"

He smiled, thought a minute, and said, "I don't believe I can point to any particular lesson. Each season of life has its own set of problems, and we have to solve them as they come along."

At first I was disappointed because the answer had not been more specific. But I began to realize later that the answer revealed the wisdom of a pilgrimage that, as far as I'm concerned, met every criterion of success.

Perhaps you will understand why this chapter is being written on that same screened-in front porch of the old farmhouse that now is silent. It seemed only natural to conclude a book about celebrating life in a place where life was celebrated through many years. My grandparents knew the meaning of suffering, yet never in all the years I knew them do I remember their speaking a single profane word or doing an unkind deed. They believed in God, in the dignity and value of hard work, in being honest and fair with others, and in the promise of the hereafter about which Jesus spoke. They loved greatly and were greatly loved. And they left an imperishable heritage for all of us who were fortunate enough to be a part of their pilgrimage.

Reflecting on these thoughts, I recalled that Mark Van Doren once said, "Good persons know the same things." The things my grandparents had learned are the things that all serious pilgrims must learn. The laws of life are the same for everyone, and to say yes to life in its entirety is to link ourselves with forces that inevitably carry us successfully forward. By living each stage fully, we allow ourselves to experience the kinds of realities that "teach us to number our days, that we may apply our hearts unto wisdom."

A Birthday Prayer

Our Father who gives us days to number,

Today brings special meaning because it marks the beginning of another year and because it gives me the opportunity to thank you for the gift of life.

Help me to understand more clearly what it means to know that *in you* I live and move and have my being.

Remind me of those past experiences that give evidence of your providential care and of the love, kindness, and understanding of family and friends.

Then let me view the untraveled road as an opportunity to adventure zestfully, meaningfully, and productively, to be fully alive to the glory of God. And in this pause in my pilgrimage give me the insight to know and the power to do whatever is necessary to achieve your divine purpose for allowing me the sacred privilege of life.

Please accept this prayer in the name of him who came that we might have life and have it more abundantly. Amen.

LOUIS O. CALDWELL is the director of the Christian Counseling Center, and professor of psychology at Southern Bible College in Houston, Texas. A state licensed psychotherapist, Dr. Caldwell has always found time for talking and counseling with people and has a private clinical practice. He conducts married couples' retreats across the nation and teaches seminars on Christian family life in churches in the Houston area. In between rearing four children and pursuing hobbies as diversified as piloting a private plane and playing softball, he has become a prolific and popular inspirational writer, communicating sound Christian counseling through the written word.

OTHER BOOKS BY LOUIS O. CALDWELL

The Adventure of Becoming One
Meditations for Modern Marrieds
After the Tassel is Moved
Another Tassel is Moved
Meditations for College Students
Miracles of the Master
Parables of the Master
When Partners Become Parents
Speaker's Source Book for Talks to Teens
Through the Years